PET OWNER'S GUIDE TO THE
MINIATURE SCHNAUZER

Pat Kidd

RINGPRESS

ABOUT THE AUTHOR

Pat Kidd first owned Great Danes, but decided she wanted a groomed breed that presented more of a challenge in the show ring.

Pat has owned and bred top-winning Mini Schnauzers for a number of years. She owned Ch. Dashing Dixie Dean, and is the breeder of litter brother and sister Champions Amurus Ansome Arry and Amurus Adorable Adora.

Pat was the secretary of the Miniature Schnauzer Club for five years, and sits on the committee. She is a Championship Show judge for Miniature Schnauzers and Schnauzers.

ACKNOWLEDGEMENTS

The publisher would like to thank Judith Childerley (Childgait Miniature Schnauzers) and Caroline Wareing (Caskayd Kennels) for their help with photography.

Designed by: Rob Benson

Published by Ringpress Books Limited,
PO Box 8, Lydney, Gloucestershire,
GL15 4YN, United Kingdom.

First published 2001
©2001 Ringpress Books Limited. All rights reserved

ISBN 1 86054 144 5

Printed and bound in Hong Kong through Printworks International Ltd.

CONTENTS

INTRODUCING THE MINIATURE SCHNAUZER   6

German origins; Breed roots; Early Minis;
The breed in Britain; The breed in America;
Colours; UK breed clubs; American breed
clubs; German breed clubs; Breed character.

CHOOSING A   12
MINIATURE SCHNAUZER

Taking responsibility; Grooming needs;
Rescue Schnauzers; Buying a puppy;
Docking; Ask the breeder; Breeder support;
Breeding potential; Dog or bitch?; Colour;
Home-rearing; Kennelled litter; Picking a pup; One or two?;
Show pup; Preparing for the pup (Puppy-proofing;
Shopping list).

PUPPY CARE   24

Journey home; Home at last; Inoculations/worming; Toilet-
training; Family introductions; Daily routine; Feeding;
Early lessons (Name-calling; Teaching "No"; House rules;
Handling; Positive play); Exercise needs; Teething; Dental
care; Brushing teeth; Ear development.

TRAINING AND   38
SOCIALISING

Using commands; Training tips;
Controlling barking; Dominant
behaviour; Lead-training; Sit;
Down; Stay; Come/Recall;
Heel; Socialisation; Puppy
parties; Training classes;
Advanced training.

5 ADULT CARE 48

Diet (Feeding scraps; Meat; Canned; Complete); Exercise; Veteran Care (Veteran diet); Euthanasia.

6 GROOMING 52

Puppy grooming (Removing the puppy coat); Adult coat care (Combing; Eyebrows; Beard; Ears; Clipping; Stripping/Raking); General checks (Teeth; Ears; Feet).

7 SHOWING YOUR MINATURE SCHNAUZER 62

The Breed Standard (Temperament; General appearance; Head; Ears; Eyes; Mouth; Neck; Forequarters; Body; Tail; Legs; Feet; Gait/Movement; Coat; Colour; Size; American differences); Getting Started Best presentations; Natural show dog; Learning gait; Handling; The show stance; Puppy class; Rules.

8 HEALTH CARE 68

Administering medicine; Preventative care (Vaccinations; Worming); Accidents (Bee stings; Heatstroke; Cuts; Burns); Breed-prone conditions (Eye conditions; Haemorrhagic gastroenteritis; Kidney failure; Diabetes; Addison's disease; Cushings disease; Schnauzer bumps).

1 Introducing The Miniature Schnauzer

The Miniature Schnauzer is the smallest of the Schnauzer family. At approximately 14 inches (35.6 cms) at the shoulder, the Miniature is towered over by his cousins – the Standard Schnauzer at 19 inches (47.5 cms), and the Giant Schnauzer, where males measure up to 27.5 inches (70 cms).

GERMAN ORIGINS

The Standard Schnauzer is the oldest member of the Schnauzer family, and there are paintings depicting Schnauzer-like dogs as far back as the 15th century.

The Standard can be traced back to Bavaria and Württemberg, the area where many cattle dogs originate.

The Miniature Schnauzer is a relatively new breed.

The Standard Schnauzer was also a cattle dog, guarding stable and yard. He also showed great prowess as an excellent ratter.

BREED ROOTS

Many people have speculated about the background of the Miniature Schnauzer, which is a relatively new breed, appearing in the latter part of the 19th century.

Contrary to popular beliefs the Miniature Schnauzer is not the product of breeding with small Schnauzers, but it has been the result of careful breeding of Schnauzers crossed with Affenpinschers. Some people believe that Poodles or even Spitz-type dogs can be found in the Mini's origins.

EARLY MINIS

In the early days, the Mini's appearance resembled the dogs we have today, but, as with all breeds, changes have gradually occurred over the years.

The original Minis had harsh coats and most had cut (cropped) ears and shortened tails. Their beards were shorter, as were the furnishings (leg hair), and the colours varied. Apparently, Minis came in many colours, as there is mention of reds, black and tans, yellows, whites, pepper-and-salts, and parti-colours.

THE BREED IN BRITAIN

The Miniature Schnauzer was first seen in the United Kingdom during the late 1920s. From Holland, a Mr Hancock imported a black bitch called Enstone Gerti van Duinslut. A couple of years later, he imported two more – Dutch Champion Enstone Ador van Rheinstolz and Enstone Barbel von Dinghaus.

The breed was slow to gain popularity (which is not always a bad thing). In the early years, Miniature Schnauzers were registered with Standard Schnauzers. The granting of Challenge Certificates (certificates which make up a Champion in the show ring) did not happen until the Miniature was recognised in its own right in 1935.

Interestingly, in 1935 the name was changed to Affenschnauzer – reflecting the fact that the Miniature Schnauzer was created by crossing a Standard Schnauzer with an Affenpinscher. It is under the Affenschnauzer name that the Kennel Club Stud Book listed the winners of Challenge Certificates (CCs).

However, the change of name

did not please everyone and Germany soon protested, so, in 1936, the name Miniature Schnauzer was reinstated.

THE BREED IN AMERICA

Miniature Schnauzers arrived in America in the 1920s, just a few years before their arrival in England. W. Goff from Massachusetts imported a dog and a bitch from a Mr Krappatsch. This breeder sold two more Minis,

In the United States, the breed generally has cropped ears.

to Marie Lewis, also in Massachusetts, and it was then that the breed really began to establish itself in the US.

Like their counterparts in England, the first imports had to be registered with Standard Schnauzers which, when first imported, were known as Wire-haired Pinschers.

But changes were afoot and it was not too long before the Miniature and the Standard Schnauzer were able to compete as separate breeds instead of against each other. The year 1926 saw not only the split of the two sizes, but the name was changed from Wire-haired Pinscher to Schnauzer. So, at the 1927 Combined Terrier Clubs' Specialty Show, not only were Miniature and Standard Schnauzers shown in separate classes for the first time, but also under the Schnauzer name.

During these earlier years, the height limit for Miniature Schnauzers was set at 12 inches, but gradually increased to 14 inches, the same height as their fellow Miniatures in the UK.

Originally, all Schnauzers in America – Giant, Standard and Miniature – came under the banner of the Working Group, but, in 1927, the Standard and the

Miniature Schnauzer were transferred to the Terrier Group.

For the next four years, Miniature and Standard Schnauzers were allowed to have separate best awards in each size, allowing a representative of each size to compete with each other; only one best dog – either Miniature or Standard (but not both) – could go forward to compete in the Group.

Then, in 1933, another rule change by the American Kennel Club brought about the original state of affairs whereby separate best awards were made for the Miniature and the Standard, and so, once again, the two sizes were to compete in the Group.

COLOURS

Many newcomers to the breed presume that black is a relatively new colour in the breed, but the Breed Standard has always recognised the pepper-and-salt shades and black colours. But it is the pepper-and-salt which is the more prolific colour and which has dominated the show ring, on both sides of the Atlantic.

Although black Miniature Schnauzers have always been around (as long ago as 1936 America made breed history by

Black Minis are currently enjoying a revival of interest.

producing the first black Champion: Ch. Cunning Asta of Bambivin), black has never quite gained the popularity of the pepper-and-salt colouring. Recently, there has been a revived interest in black coats, however, with several exciting black imports and Champions.

During the 1970s, black-and-silver Schnauzers appeared. Although, at that time, it was not a colour recognised by the Kennel Club, the black-and-silver combination proved so popular that it eventually gained recognition in 1985. The first black-and-silver Champion was seen the following year, when Ch. Qassaba Tia Crystal gained her title.

UK BREED CLUBS

There is only one Miniature Schnauzer Club specialising solely in Miniature Schnauzers. However, there are other clubs, which cater for all three sizes of the Schnauzer family.

The British Miniature Schnauzer Club was formed in 1933 and changed its name in 1935 to the British Affenschnauzer Club. After changing back to the original name in 1936, it was disbanded for various reasons, including lack of money and enthusiasts.

The Schnauzer Club of Great Britain (which was formed in 1929) then became the custodian of Miniature Schnauzers. In 1953, The Miniature Schnauzer Club was formed and is still flourishing today, thanks to the growing popularity of the Miniature Schnauzer and the breed's enthusiastic owners.

AMERICAN BREED CLUBS

In America, the original club formed to look after the interests of Miniature Schnauzers was the Wire-haired Pinscher Club (as Schnauzers were then known).

This club, which was formed in 1925, was responsible for both Miniature and Standard Schnauzer welfare.

In the early 1930s, the American Kennel Club ruled that Specialty Clubs should cover only the interests of one breed. Miniature Schnauzer enthusiasts felt that this decision could have a damaging effect on Miniatures, as the rule change implied that Miniature and Standard Schnauzers were in fact the same breed, opening the door to mating the two sizes with each other. To look after and to ensure the future of the Mini, the Miniature Schnauzer Club of America was formed in 1933.

Being the parent organisation, this club is consulted on matters concerning Miniature Schnauzers and helped to bring about the change in the Mini Schnauzer height (from 12 inches to 14 inches).

GERMAN BREED CLUBS

Nowadays, the Pinscher-Schnauzer Club is responsible for the interests of Affenpinschers, Miniature Schnauzers, Pinschers, and Schnauzers (Minis, Standards, and Giant).

Originally, the Pinscher Club was formed at Cologne in 1895, looking after the interests of both the wire-haired Schnauzer and the smooth-haired Pinscher. Later, in

A friendly, confident dog, the Miniature Schnauzer will also be a useful guard.

1901, the Bavarian Schnauzer Club was formed in Munich. In 1918, both clubs combined to form the Pinscher-Schnauzer Club of today.

BREED CHARACTER

Friendly, amusing and outgoing, the Miniature Schnauzer's personality plays an important part in his popularity.

He has an easy-going temperament, and a tendency towards being vocal rather than aggressive. In his duty as your self-appointed home 'guard dog', he will bark to warn you of strangers, rather than to attack.

Ultimately, the Miniature Schnauzer is a companion dog who adores human contact, craves attention, and loves to please. There is no doubt, he makes the ideal dog for most families.

Choosing A Miniature Schnauzer

B efore committing yourself and your family to the responsibility of looking after a Miniature Schnauzer, make sure you do some research. Will a Miniature Schnauzer fit in with your family's lifestyle? Will *you* fit in with the Miniature Schnauzer?

TAKING RESPONSIBILITY

Anyone who has owned a dog will tell you of the enormous enjoyment it can bring. But along with the pleasure comes the responsibility.

All aspects of ownership should be considered. Who will be responsible for the daily grooming of your Miniature Schnauzer (see below)? Are you prepared to pay for annual vaccinations and veterinary fees for the next 14 years or so? Where will your Mini stay when you go on holiday? Will your relatives agree to look after your pet? Will you place him in a suitable boarding kennels?

It takes a lot of hard work to keep the Miniature Schnauzer's coat in order.

Talk to your family to make sure everyone is committed to looking after a dog. You should also find out what it is really like to share your life with a Mini – talk to other owners, and visit as many breeders as possible before making the commitment. Please don't buy a puppy on the spur of the moment; a dead-cute puppy can be irresistible, but could become a very expensive, heartbreaking mistake.

GROOMING NEEDS

Miniature Schnauzers are a groomed breed. This means that, although the Miniature Schnauzer coat does not moult, it still grows, and therefore requires combing, clipping or stripping (plucking the hair out).

When groomed correctly, the Miniature Schnauzer is a very smart-looking breed, with his long beard, bushy eyebrows, harsh, wiry coat (when hand-stripped) and profuse leg hair. Most people find this appearance irresistible. But, it is only achieved with hard work and a strict grooming regime.

People are also under the misguided impression that Minis only need stripping or clipping twice a year, and that puppies

should not be groomed until they are six months of age – this is wrong. The Mini will require between six and eight clips/strips each year.

Additionally, a puppy should be groomed on a daily basis (just for a few minutes). You may think this sounds rather extreme, but there is nothing more traumatic for a four- to six-month-old Miniature Schnauzer than being groomed for the first time.

RESCUE SCHNAUZERS

Not everyone wants a puppy, so that only leaves a couple of options – you either ask the breeder if there are any older dogs for sale, or you contact a breed rescue organisation. Your national breed club will have details of organisations acting on its behalf and can supply the names and telephone numbers.

With a breed rescue, the choice of dogs available is rather more limited than if you were picking a puppy – you may have to stay on a waiting list for some time until a suitable dog becomes available. The rescue organisation will do its very best to match you to a dog that best suits your lifestyle, surroundings and experience. Your home and environment will be checked in an attempt to ensure the Miniature Schnauzer will never need rehoming again.

BUYING A PUPPY

It is always advisable to buy a pedigree dog directly from a recognised breeder, even though reputable breeders may have a waiting list.

Visit a dog show which has classes for Miniature Schnauzers, talk to the exhibitors, and get some hands-on experience of the breed. Telephone your national kennel club which will be able to give you contact details of breed club secretaries, who, in turn, will be able to recommend breeders.

These breeders may not have any puppies when you call, but you will be able to visit and talk to them before making that all-important decision to take on a Miniature Schnauzer.

DOCKING

Nowadays, not all Miniature Schnauzers in the UK have their tails docked, but most breeders continue to have their puppies docked by a veterinary surgeon at

Visit a show to get first-hand experience of the breed.

three to four days. Talk to the breeder before the litter is born if you have any preference towards docking.

ASK THE BREEDER

As well as establishing your docking preferences, ask the breeder if the adults have been eye-tested. Ask to see the relevant paperwork. Will the puppies be litter-screened for any eye abnormalities before you take your Mini home? Again, check the paperwork.

Make a list of any questions you wish to ask, so you don't forget anything you would like to know. The breeder is also likely to have many questions to pose to you. A responsible breeder will want to vet you and your family thoroughly, but don't be offended – the breeder is concerned that the puppy is going to a suitable home.

You will be asked questions about your family, dog experience, and lifestyle. Should this not be the case, then be a little wary, as you may not receive any after-service from this breeder.

BREEDER SUPPORT

After-sales advice is an important part of the breeder's service. You are likely to have many questions

in the first few months after taking your puppy home. Responsible breeders will be more than happy to advise you on a whole host of issues.

They should also be genuinely interested to know how their puppies are progressing, and, if you experience any unforeseen problems, they should offer to take the puppy back to rehome him.

BREEDING POTENTIAL

If you are thinking of breeding from the puppy you are purchasing, be honest with the breeder, as he/she may feel the puppy you choose is not of good enough quality.

In some instances, breeders place a breeding block on a puppy's registration. This means that, if someone breeds from this 'blocked' dog, the puppies would not be allowed to be registered with your kennel club.

DOG OR BITCH?

Most people have a preconceived idea about whether they want a dog or a bitch. Very often, they can remember a family pet years ago that was of a particular sex.

For those of you who have not owned a dog before, my advice

Males tend to be fairly bold and outgoing.

Dogs and bitches both like their home comforts, and adore being with the family, making the Miniature Schnauzer a most loyal pet.

If you decide on a bitch, you will have to consider the regular inconvenience of 'seasons'. These will start at from six to nine months of age and continue throughout the bitch's life at six-monthly intervals, unless you make the decision to have the bitch spayed.

The bitch will bleed for 14 to 21 days, and the vulva will swell. As the season progresses, the bleeding

would be to keep an open mind. This way, you will have a better chance of finding your ideal puppy sooner. Remember, litters vary, and no-one can predict the number or sex of the puppies, so you might have to wait a long time before you find the puppy of your choice.

I find Miniature Schnauzer dogs and bitches to be as loving as one another. Both enjoy their food (so watch the diet), but I have to admit my personal preference is a dog, purely because dogs are generally a little more outgoing than bitches, who are often more laid-back.

Bitches are generally more laid-back than dogs.

will reduce and the colour will fade. Your bitch is most receptive to dogs around the tenth to twelfth day (this is a guideline only). During her season, your bitch will have to be isolated from all other dogs, or you will run the risk of her being mated.

If your choice is a dog, then you will not have the inconvenience of seasons, but some people say dogs will mark their territory. However, I have found that only prolific stud dogs have a tendency to do this.

COLOUR
It is very rare that Miniature Schnauzer breeders have all three colours, so if you have a preference for a particular colour, make sure you discuss this with the breeders.

Pepper-and-salt is the more usual colour, so you will probably have a greater choice of pups. Blacks are becoming more popular, but black-and-silvers still seem to be in the minority.

Occasionally, you will see a white Miniature Schnauzer. They are not albinos, as they do have good eye and nose pigment, but they are not recognised by the Kennel Club or the American Kennel Club.

PEPPER-AND-SALT
A distinctive colouring which is due to each harsh hair being individually banded – i.e. each hair has three colours from light to dark grey.

All colours of pepper-and-salt are acceptable in even proportions.

Pepper-and-salt is the most common colour.

The eyebrows, beard, cheeks, leg hair furnishings (not higher than the elbow on the front, and not on the thigh on the rear), under the body (not higher than the elbow), under the tail, and the inside rear legs, will all be a silver-white colour.

BLACK-AND-SILVER

Solid black except for the eyebrows, beard, cheeks, leg hair furnishings (not higher than the elbow on the front, and not on the thigh on the rear), under the body (not higher than the elbow), under the tail, and the inside rear legs, which will all be a silver-white colour.

BLACK

Pure black with no red, grey or white hair.

HOME-REARING

Hopefully, the litter of puppies you have chosen will be reared in the home, giving them the advantage of already being accustomed to many household noises, being handled by the family, and generally being well socialised.

The litter should be kept in clean conditions, and look healthy, bright-eyed and outgoing. Look for signs of ill health – runny eyes, a poor dull coat, and faeces that are not well formed are all warning signs, and any litter exhibiting these signs should be avoided.

KENNELLED LITTER

If the litter is reared in kennels, they may be a bit more shy than a litter that is reared in the home, but the conditions and surroundings should still be immaculate and the puppies should look just as healthy.

You may find that a kennel puppy requires a bit more understanding and patience, but

The mother's temperament will give you some indication of how the puppies will turn out.

The puppies should be clean, healthy, and inquisitive.

should soon acclimatise to his new home and surroundings if provided with thorough and ongoing socialisation.

PICKING A PUP

Between four to six weeks, you will be able to see the puppies. Be wary if you are invited to see the puppies before this time, as it could indicate lack of experience by the breeder (as the pups are vulnerable to infection).

Temperament should be the first thing you consider when choosing a puppy from a litter.

If you have a large family, don't pick a puppy that is quiet, and who backs away or sits in the corner; a bold, confident pup would be a better choice.

As well as assessing the Minis yourself, talk to the breeder who will know all the puppies' individual temperaments.

If, after you have walked into the room, one particular puppy hasn't tugged at your heartstrings, then sit with the litter, and watch them interacting. It won't be long before a pup grabs your attention.

ONE OR TWO?

Do not be tempted into buying two puppies, which could spell double the trouble. Training and grooming a puppy is a time-consuming business, and it will be difficult to cope with two at the same time. Also, puppies tend to bond with each other, and you will be missing out on that special

The breeder will help you to assess show potential.

rapport you build with your new puppy in the early stages of his life with you. It is much more sensible to wait until your puppy is a little older and then, if you still wish to have another, do so.

SHOW PUP

If you are looking for a show dog, go to as many shows as possible, look at all the exhibits, and buy catalogues, so that you can study as many Miniature Schnauzers as possible. Decide what type of look you like, and talk to the breeders.

However, remember that no-one can guarantee that an eight-week-old puppy will become a quality show dog, as so many things can go wrong.

If the dog doesn't make the grade, you must be prepared to care for your Mini for the rest of his life.

PREPARING FOR THE PUP
So, the day is fast approaching, and soon you will be bringing your pup home, but first you must consider the puppy's safety.

PUPPY-PROOFING
Are there are any gaps under the fence that the puppy could get under? Will the puppy have access to a part of the garden where the milkman, postman etc. may leave a gate open? Give thought to any prized plants, and move them to a part of the garden where the puppy cannot gain access.

Your home and garden should be completely safe before your puppy arrives home.

Give some thought to the areas to which your Mini will be allowed access. Make sure all hazards (such as electrical wires etc.) are safely out of his reach. Do not allow the puppy to use the stairs, as he could slip and hurt himself. It is advisable to buy a stair-gate so your Mini puppy cannot come to any harm.

SHOPPING LIST

BOWLS
Buy a feeding and water bowl in readiness for your puppy's arrival. There is a variety on the market.

A light, plastic bowl may get chipped or tipped over, and it may prove difficult to eat from if it slips around the kitchen floor. Heavy crockery bowls are usually long-lasting, but may get broken.

Alternatively, you might like to choose a metal bowl which has a small stand. Metal is long-lasting, and, with the stand, spillage will be kept to a minimum. Whatever bowls you choose, make sure they are non-slip.

COLLAR AND LEAD
You will require a collar that is approximately two inches larger than the puppy's neck. Correctly fitted, you should be able to place

two fingers between the collar and the puppy's neck.

A lightweight nylon collar and lead will be adequate, but do make sure the lead isn't going to cut into your hands when you start training your puppy.

A heavier, leather collar and lead can be bought when your Mini is older. Remember to check the collar regularly – puppies grow quickly, and the collar will need to be adjusted.

You will also need an identity tag, with the pup's name and your telephone number and address.

TOYS

There are many toys on the market. Whatever you decide to buy, remember that puppies are destructive until they have finished teething, so check that the toys are strong and safe, and check them regularly. If there is any sign of damage, replace them.

CAR SAFETY

You may wish to buy a crate for your dog to travel in (see below). Alternatively, you can invest in a car harness, which is like a seatbelt for dogs, and allows the dog to sit or lie on the seat.

DOG CHEWS

Puppies have a tendency to chew, and gnawing on the wrong things can be bad for their health – and for your pocket! Be prepared by puppy-proofing your home (see page 21) and by buying some safe chews. These will help to massage the gums and to clean tartar from the teeth (preventing bad breath).

For safety's sake, a chew should

A crate is a wise investment for the new puppy owner.

It does not take a puppy long to accept his 'den'.

be larger than your dog's mouth. Roast bones and smoked ones taste good and last a long time, but they can stain the carpet. Sterilised bones are cleaner.

Nylon and thermal plastic chews are long-lasting. Rawhide chews are very popular, cheap and fun. It is advisable to supervise your Mini with rawhide chews, as they can cause stomach upsets in puppies.

Long-lasting rope chews can help with teething. Dampen and freeze them to help relieve teething pain. They will also help to 'floss' teeth when he is older.

Check chews regularly. If there is any sign of splintering, remove and replace them.

BED/CRATE

Your Miniature Schnauzer puppy should have his own bed. This can be a cardboard box to begin with, a basket, or maybe a wire crate or cage.

Crates may sound unwelcoming places, but they are indispensable. To ensure your puppy is safe, you can close the crate door when you are unable to supervise him.

You must get the right size for your Miniature Schnauzer (a size of 24 ins x 18 ins x 20 ins/60 cms x 45 cms x 50 cms is recommended). Put in some soft fleecy veterinary bedding, and perhaps buy a cover for the cage (or put a blanket over) so your puppy can sleep draught-free at night.

A crate is collapsible, allowing you to fold it away and take it with you on holiday or when visiting friends or relatives etc.

Puppy Care

The day has finally arrived: your puppy is eight weeks old, is fully weaned, and is ready for collection.

Take a piece of fleecy veterinary bedding or a blanket, and some absorbent tissue, in case your puppy is sick on the journey home. The breeder should give you the puppy's pedigree, registration form, diet sheet, inoculation certificate and worming details, and a sample of the food your puppy is used to eating (sudden changes in diet can cause diarrhoea).

JOURNEY HOME
No matter what distance you have to travel to pick up your puppy, take someone with you. That way, your Miniature Schnauzer can snuggle up on a blanket on someone's lap on the way home. Remember, your puppy may feel very bewildered leaving his familiar home environment, so will need to feel secure.

If it is not possible for someone to accompany you, then a cage will be the best way for the puppy to travel. Put a blanket inside so the puppy is comfortable, and tie the crate to the inside of the car so that it does not move around.

Do not, under any circumstances, put your Mini on a car seat on his own. He could easily fall off, or cause you to have an accident. Nor should you contemplate putting the pup in the boot/trunk. Not only is it cruel, but the temperatures in the boot could soar, and kill your new puppy.

Always make sure the car is well ventilated when your puppy is inside, and never leave him unattended in the car.

HOME AT LAST
Let your puppy investigate his new sleeping quarters, which should be

The big day arrives when it is time to take your puppy home.

draught-free and in a quiet part of the house. Whether it is a basket or a cage, encourage him to lie on his new bed. Remember, this is to be his little den, and his privacy and property should be respected. Teach the family (children in particular) that, when the puppy has retired to his bed, he should be left undisturbed.

Make sure you place lots of newspaper around the bedding area, as your puppy may not be able to hold his water for too long.

Take your Mini outside to investigate the garden. If he happens to perform while there, give praise so that, right from the outset, he will know that this is the right place to go to the toilet. (See page 26.)

INOCULATIONS/WORMING
When you get your Mini home, make an appointment to see your veterinary surgeon to discuss an immunisation and worming programme as soon as you can.

Give your puppy a chance to explore his new surroundings.

(See Chapter Eight for more information.)

Until your puppy has been immunised, you will have to keep him in the confines of your garden. He must not come into contact with any unfamiliar dogs, nor should he be exercised in an area where other dogs have been, as he may catch a fatal illness.

TOILET-TRAINING

House-training your Mini can start immediately. Remember that your pup is still a baby and cannot go for any length of time without emptying his bladder and bowels.

He will need to be taken outdoors as soon as he wakes up, immediately after a meal, and before bedtime. You should also be aware of the warning signs – a pup that starts sniffing the floor, often circling, is usually desperate to relieve himself.

Your Miniature Schnauzer's natural instinct to be clean will not develop if the opportunity isn't there. In other words, if you don't take your puppy outside to eliminate, nature forces the puppy to relieve himself indoors, and this will soon become a habit that is difficult to break.

PUPPY CARE

ELIMINATION PROCESS

Take your puppy out to a particular spot in the garden that you have chosen to be his toileting area. Stay with him; if you leave your Mini outside on his own, he will feel abandoned and will just sit there hoping someone will come and rescue him. Then, as soon as he gets into the house, he is likely to promptly relieve himself!

When he starts to eliminate, use a command word or phrase, such as "Wee wees" or "Be clean". Be consistent with the command you use, and give lots of praise and a treat when your puppy has performed.

PAPER-TRAINING

In the house, put plenty of newspaper on the floor so that it is difficult for your Mini not to go on paper. Gradually, reduce the amount of paper until there is just a small amount by the door. When your Mini approaches the paper, take him outside.

ACCIDENTS HAPPEN

If your Mini has an accident in the house, don't be cross – he is only answering a call of nature. If you catch him in the act, say "No!" sternly or clap your hands to distract his attention and to stop him mid-flow. Then, take him outside.

Don't ever tell your puppy off after the event, as he won't have a clue why you are angry, and will not associate it with something he did earlier.

FAMILY INTRODUCTIONS

CHILDREN

Establish your puppy's position in the household as soon as you get him home, and teach him to respect all members of the family, including children.

Also, teach the children to respect your Miniature Schnauzer: they must never be allowed to pick up the puppy, unless supervised, and then only when the child is sitting down, so the pup cannot be dropped by accident.

Children should also be taught not to pull the beard or eyebrows, no matter how tempting, and the sharing of food, is also a big 'no-no'. Not only is it unhygienic, but Miniature Schnauzer milk teeth are extremely sharp and the exuberant pup may bite a child's fingers by mistake.

It is important that playtime with the puppy and children should always be supervised.

If you already have a dog at home, be tactful when introducing the new arrival.

OTHER PETS

Introducing a puppy to an existing dog or cat should always be done under supervision. Do not let the puppy get too excited, as his exuberance could irritate your cat or dog.

Until you are certain that your animals will mix without any skirmishes, do not leave them alone, and never feed them together. If in any doubt, put your puppy safely in his crate when you are unable to supervise them.

DAILY ROUTINE

From the very first day, create a routine for your puppy. Your Miniature Schnauzer will require four meals a day, and this will help to establish the general routine.

MORNING

- On waking, take your puppy outside to relieve himself (see page 26).
- Breakfast: a small bowl of wheat-based cereal, with warm milk.
- Take the puppy outside again and wait for him to go to the toilet. When he does, praise him and tell him what a good puppy he is.
- Playtime.
- Take the puppy outside again.
- Playtime should be followed by

PUPPY CARE

In no time, a friendship between puppy and adult will develop.

rest. Make sure that every member of the family realises that puppies need their sleep and should not be disturbed.
- Take the puppy outside when he wakes up as he is likely to need to relieve himself once more.

AFTERNOON
- Lunch: a small amount of complete food, soaked until soft. As your puppy gets older, the food may be left dry. Alternatively, you can feed minced (chopped) meat, or a sixth of a tin of puppy food, together with a small amount of small-sized mixer or dried puppy food.
- Take your puppy outside to relieve himself.
- Playtime, followed by rest.

- Tea, as above, or feed with rice or pasta (approximately $2/3$ oz).
- Take the puppy outside to relieve himself.

EVENING
- Supper: either two to three tablespoonfuls of rice pudding, a scrambled egg, warm milk with a biscuit, or half a pint of milk with cereal.
- Take your Mini outside to relieve himself, before settling him in his bed.

FEEDING
Your dog's diet is the key to keeping him fit, healthy and happy.
  If you are planning on feeding your dog a home-made diet, you will need to study the nutritional benefits of this diet, and you may

need to use vitamin supplements to ensure a complete balanced diet. Talk to your Mini's breeder and your vet for advice on the essential nutrients needed in a healthy, well-balanced diet.

If you choose to feed tinned food, read the label carefully – not all tinned food is nutritionally complete and some will require a mixer biscuit. Either way, it should be clearly stated on the label.

Many owners prefer to feed a dried food, as it is less messy and more convenient. There are many complete dried foods on the market to suit all budgets. You should be able to find a suitable product for your dog's lifestyle and age.

As the name suggests, complete food is exactly that – it contains the correct balance of nutrients necessary for your dog, and you should not add any supplements.

There is a variety of diets for the different stages of your dog's life. Growing puppies require more calories, protein, minerals and vitamins than an adult dog. Puppies should be fed on a growth diet until they reach maturity. An adult Miniature Schnauzer will require a maintenance diet, with a moderate amount of calories, protein, vitamins and minerals.

Your Mini puppy should always have access to clean, fresh water at all times.

DIETARY DIFFICULTIES

If your puppy develops loose bowels, monitor him carefully. Cut out one of his meals. At his next mealtime, feed a small amount of chicken and boiled rice. You could also try a couple of arrowroot biscuits in water. Do not give any milk, as this has a tendency to exacerbate the problem.

If your Mini does not return to normal within a short space of time, or if there is ever any blood in the faeces, consult your veterinary surgeon immediately.

CHANGING DIETS

If you decide you do not want to feed the same diet to your Mini that the breeder had been using, any change of diet must be done gradually over a five- to ten-day period. Mix the new diet with your puppy's former food, gradually increasing the proportion until only the new diet remains.

To evaluate your puppy's new diet, watch for any changes in the volume and consistency of faeces, condition of the skin and hair, and the general demeanour of your

It is important to feed a balanced diet to a growing puppy.

puppy. If his overall condition seems to deteriorate, discuss your Mini's diet with your vet.

TREATS

If your puppy is receiving a complete balanced diet, it will be unnecessary to feed tidbits. However, treats can be used as rewards as part of training. Fresh, raw vegetables can be beneficial, but avoid chocolate unless it is a proprietary dog treat, as chocolate intended for human use is very toxic to dogs.

Remember, don't feed treats or give chews at family mealtimes as this will lead to begging and other antisocial behaviour.

OBESITY

Miniature Schnauzers love their grub, so be careful that yours doesn't become overweight. If he does become obese (which is unhealthy for your dog), cut down on the amount of food at mealtimes and reduce the number of treats. If in doubt, ask your vet for advice; many surgeries hold special weight-loss clinics.

CUTTING DOWN MEALS

From approximately three months of age, your puppy will probably begin to lose interest in one of his milk meals. This is usual, and you can reduce the number of meals to three a day.

From six months of age, your Miniature Schnauzer pup can be on two meals a day, and, by the time he has reached eight months, you can cut down to just one meal a day, if you wish. I have always fed two meals a day, at lunchtime and teatime, but you can fit meals in with your plans.

EARLY LESSONS

NAME-CALLING

Choose a name that is easy to say, and repeat it over and over until your puppy recognises it. Talk comfortingly to your puppy while using his new name – he should associate his name with enjoyable experiences, such as being petted or given a treat.

TEACHING "NO"

If your Miniature Schnauzer does something you disapprove of, tell him "No!". Use a stern tone of voice, and your puppy will understand that he has done something naughty.

Don't wag your finger at your Mini, as a young puppy will not know what it means and may think you are playing.

Remember to use your puppy's name at every opportunity.

Never hit your puppy; it is a completely wasted exercise, and will ruin any rapport you have built with your Mini. Always train your dog with kindness, and reward him when he does something right.

HOUSE RULES

The first few months of your puppy's life will be when he establishes his relationship with his new family. Be consistent and firm, while providing a secure and loving home.

The whole family should be aware of the house rules and adhere to them. For example, if the puppy is not allowed access to a particular part of the garden or house, then everyone should be reminded to keep doors and gates shut. Or, if your Mini is not allowed on the furniture, no-one should ever let him break the rules. Any visiting friends or family should also be made aware of the house rules.

HANDLING

Your puppy is going to find his first examination by the vet a little unsettling, so try to alleviate his anxiety. Rehearse the situation: place him on a non-slip mat on the table, and practise looking at his mouth, eyes, ears and tail. All rewards and punishment must be immediate. Puppies only associate rewards with the most recent behaviour, so, if rewards are too late, then they are ineffective.

POSITIVE PLAY

There's no reason why early training cannot be introduced into your puppy's play sessions. With the use of chews and toys, teach your puppy to understand "Sit", "Come", "Down" and to get used to the collar and lead (see Chapter Four).

During your pup's play, you should always be in control: if your Mini gets overexcited, calm things down (e.g. take away the toys and just talk to your puppy). I hate to see people play-fighting with young puppies. You may think it is funny to encourage a puppy to bite and growl, but when the dog is older you'll regret teaching your puppy this extremely bad habit, so don't start it in the first place.

EXERCISE NEEDS

Your puppy will require little exercise in the first few weeks with you. Playing in the house or garden will be adequate until your Mini is fully immunised. Then,

For the first few weeks, your puppy will get all the exercise he needs playing in the garden.

take a little five-minute walk each day to get your puppy used to his collar and lead.

Over the next few weeks gradually build up the exercise to ten minutes, then fifteen minutes a day at around six months of age.

A Mini is an adaptable dog and will fit in with your lifestyle. If you enjoy long walks, your adult Mini will too, as long as the exercise he gets is built up over a gradual period.

TEETHING

Miniature Schnauzers will cut their first teeth when they are a few weeks old, and, like their owners, will get two sets of teeth. All puppy teeth are present by eight weeks of age, and they set the pathway for the permanent teeth to follow.

Your Miniature Schnauzer should have all his permanent teeth at six months of age. Throughout this time, you should check the teeth to make sure the milk teeth are not being retained, and to spot any abnormalities.

While teething, your puppy's gums will be sore, and he may need to chew to relieve the pain from his tender gums. Hopefully, you will have already provided your puppy with lots of playthings and chews to help keep him occupied. If he doesn't have adequate things to gnaw, he will find his own chews – your slippers, your sofa etc.

To help relieve the pain further, some owners rub the gums with a proprietary brand of gum-soother to alleviate any discomfort.

DENTAL CARE

When looking at your puppy's mouth, a general guide is that no two teeth of the same type should occupy the same place at the same time. If you don't get this corrected at an early stage,

Provide safe toys for your puppy to chew, particularly when he starts teething.

permanent damage to the dental pattern may occur, so consult your vet if you have any concerns about your Mini's mouth.

As we care for our dogs better and they live longer, daily dental care is more necessary than ever. A sad statistic is that more than 85 per cent of dogs aged four years and over have periodontal disease. You wouldn't think of neglecting your own teeth, so, in order to prevent the build-up of plaque, daily brushing will help to prevent gum disease and tooth loss.

If the plaque is allowed to stay on your dog's teeth, it becomes mineralised and is called tartar. Unlike plaque, this cannot be removed by brushing, and a trip to the veterinary surgeon will be necessary to remove the tartar.

Obviously, prevention is better than cure, so make sure your Mini has plenty of chews (it is the action of chewing that cleans the teeth) and ensure that his teeth are brushed daily.

Keep a close check on your puppy during the vulnerable growing period.

BRUSHING TEETH

Nowadays, there are plenty of proprietary brands of toothpaste and toothbrushes for the dog. Never use toothpaste intended for human use; instead, buy specially-prepared canine paste, which is usually meat-flavoured. You will require a soft brush with a relatively long handle.

After your dog's last meal of the day, apply a little toothpaste to the brush and gently brush around your Mini's mouth to remove any food around the teeth and gums. Don't overdo the brushing or you may make the gums sore.

EAR DEVELOPMENT

During this teething period, you may notice that your Mini's ears start to 'fly'. This is where, instead of falling forward to the corner of the eye, the ear flap is carried quite far back. Sometimes, the ears may even look as though they are totally erect.

Thankfully, not all Miniature Schnauzers suffer in this way and you may not notice anything wrong with your puppy's ears.

Should the ears alter in appearance though, you could, while your puppy is on your lap, gently massage the ear at the base.

4 *Training And Socialising*

Miniature Schnauzers are reliable, alert, intelligent dogs who adore their human companions. With kind words and a lot of patience, your Miniature Schnauzer can be taught good manners and simple obedience in no time at all.

As soon as you get your Miniature Schnauzer pup home, you can begin to teach him very basic obedience, and get him used to a collar and lead. You don't have to wait until your Mini is fully immunised – you can start to train your puppy and take him for little walks around the garden (remember not to take him out to public places until he is fully immunised).

USING COMMANDS

Never mix up your commands. For example, never tell your Mini to "Sit down" – the puppy won't know whether he should sit or lie down. If you don't want your puppy on the furniture, use the word "Off", not "Down", otherwise your puppy will think "Oh, I can lie down on the furniture."

TRAINING TIPS

- Always make training fun – use toys and treats, and make sure you are in control.
- Use a voice with authority, but don't scream or shout.
- Retain your dog's undivided attention, keeping lessons short and fun.
- If your Mini shows signs of boredom, stop the lesson.
- Always finish a lesson with some fun and games for a couple of minutes.
- Rewards must be immediate.

CONTROLLING BARKING

Miniature Schnauzers can have a tendency towards barking. This is natural for Minis, but obviously you will need to control it, as neighbours may complain.

Barking should not be discouraged totally, as it is your dog's way of letting you know that someone is about, or that something is wrong. When your Mini barks appropriately (e.g. when a visitor knocks on the door), praise him, then say "Enough", and walk him away from the situation. If the barking persists, repeat "No" in a stern voice. As soon as your Mini is quiet, use praise and perhaps give a small treat, but only if your dog is quiet and is paying attention to you. Usually, ignoring your dog's bad behaviour can be more effective than shouting, particularly when dealing with barking.

Make training sessions fun by using treats and toys.

DOMINANT BEHAVIOUR

If your Mini shows signs of dominance (i.e. he refuses to let you take away a toy or to remove his food bowl), you must stop this behaviour while he is still a youngster. Should you allow this kind of behaviour to continue, he will believe he is getting the upper hand.

You must always have the confidence in yourself and your puppy to be able to take any toy, chew, or food bowl away from your Mini; there should be no adverse reaction. To encourage your pup to give up his possessions, spend a few minutes every day practising the following exercise. Give him a toy, and, after a few minutes, gently take it from him. If he doesn't growl, give him a tasty treat, and give the toy straight back to him. All the family should practise this exercise, so that the pup learns to respect all members equally, regardless of their size, age or sex.

Dominant behaviour will usually come to the fore during grooming. You must never let your Mini growl or nibble at your hand when you are grooming him. You will have to convince your Mini that grooming is fun. It is usually the fear of the unknown that makes your puppy react this way, so don't smack or shout at him, as this sort of retribution will only compound your puppy's fear of grooming. (See Chapter Three.)

LEAD-TRAINING

Gradually introduce your Mini to a soft collar and a very light lead (see page 21). Only put them on for short periods. You could try putting a collar on just before a meal, as this will take the pup's mind off this strange contraption, and it will help him to associate the collar with an enjoyable experience.

When you first try to walk your Mini on a collar and lead, you'll probably find that he will start to buck and twist, and generally

To start lead-training, your puppy must be fitted with a lightweight collar.

Let the puppy get used to his lead by allowing it to trail. Obviously, he needs to be carefully supervised.

refuse to go anywhere. Be patient, and coax your puppy to walk beside you on a lead. Stoop forward and hold a reward out in front of him to encourage him to walk forward. After a few steps, give him the toy or treat for working so hard. Practise regularly, keeping the sessions short and fun.

Always give lots of praise when the pup walks well on the lead. Say "Walk" when he is walking well beside you, so that he learns to associate the word with the right action.

If your pup doesn't walk nicely beside you, remain calm and quiet, put him in a Sit position beside you, and try again. Never drag your puppy on the lead, or he will hate his collar and lead, and will become more stubborn and agitated.

PUBLIC LEAD-WALKING

When your Miniature Schnauzer is inoculated, and it is safe to take him out, make sure you have the collar on correctly. You should only be able to get two fingers between the collar and the dog's neck (if the collar is any more loose, the dog may be able to slip his head out of the collar).

Initially, your Miniature

Use lots of encouragement to get your puppy walking with you on the lead.

Schnauzer should only go for very short walks, to allow him to become accustomed to other people, animals and noises. Give him small rewards along the way, so that he views the big wide world as a fun, enjoyable place.

SIT

From day one, as you see your puppy sit, say "Sit", and let him know he has done well, by praising him and giving him a treat. Repeat this when you practise with your puppy in a controlled environment.

Hold a treat above your puppy's head, and he will naturally go into the Sit position.

The Down is a simple progression from the Sit exercise.

Next, hold a treat in your hand. Show it to the Mini, and he will follow it with his head in an attempt to get it. Hold the treat up, above his head, just out of his reach, and he will naturally go into the Sit position when he realises he isn't tall enough to reach it while standing up. As soon as his bottom touches the floor, say "Sit", praise him, and give him a treat.

Repeat the lesson until your Mini knows the command perfectly. Next, test him at a distance, never failing to reward when your pup does well. Eventually, you can phase out the treats, until they are given only for the fastest responses.

DOWN

By now, you should have your Mini sitting on command, so progress to the Down position should, in theory, be relatively easy.

From the Sit position, coax your Mini's front feet forward until he is down. At the same time, keep repeating the word "Down", and give plenty of praise when he responds to your command.

Alternatively, you can lure your Miniature Schnauzer into position by using a treat. Show the puppy a treat. Hold it in the middle of your fist, then put your hand on the floor. The only way your Mini will be able to get close enough to your hand to try to get at the treat is by lying on the floor. As soon as his stomach hits the ground, say "Down", give lots of praise, and give him the treat he so richly deserves.

STAY

Stand in front of your Mini, and ask him to "Sit". Take off his lead, and say "Stay" while holding your hand up, palm towards your dog. Take one step back, then step forward, praise your dog, and give him a treat. Over several practice sessions, take more steps away from your dog. Never rush it, though. For example, only take two steps away when he has mastered one step, and so on. Should your Mini move, return to him, ask him to sit, and start from the beginning.

COME/RECALL

This has to be the most important lesson you can teach your Mini. A dog that doesn't respond to "Come" could easily be involved in an accident, or he could run off and become lost.

Obviously, a confined area is the best place to start teaching your Mini the Recall. Remember, when your Mini is off the lead and is having fun, it is very tempting for him suddenly to become deaf and

Use a toy and sound really enthusiastic when teaching the Recall.

Reward a correct response with lots of praise so the pup knows he has done well.

43

continue having fun. However, you must not get angry – otherwise there will be no incentive for the puppy to come to you.

You may find it useful to carry your Mini's favourite tidbit or toy in your pocket. Get his attention by calling his name, and, when he returns, praise him. You should be really pleased that your Mini has come to you – even if you have spent half an hour calling the little critter.

If you are having a very bad time teaching your Miniature Schnauzer this command, start with just the length of the lead. Put him in the Sit position, walk around to face him, slowly back away to the length of the lead. Say his name and "Come", and gently pull on the lead to bring him towards you. When he reaches you, give lots of praise and a suitable treat.

HEEL
There is nothing worse than seeing a dog taking his owner for a walk, instead of the other way round. Walking your dog should be a pleasure for you and him.

Start in the garden, with your Mini on your left-hand side. Hold the lead in your right hand to control the movement of your Mini with your left hand.

Walk forward, leading with your left foot. Use your Mini's name, and the command (e.g. "Heel" or "Walk"). Your Mini will probably take a lunge forward, but just stop, and put him back in the Sit position to start again.

If your Mini continues to pull, say "Heel", and change direction (clockwise, so as not to bump into your Mini). As soon as your Mini walks to heel, praise him. After a few steps, stop and give him a treat.

SOCIALISATION
Socialisation is the process of introducing your puppy to the world – to other animals, people, noises and places etc. Socialisation will allow your puppy to develop a confident and pleasant personality. If he does not receive adequate socialisation, he will grow up to be afraid and timid, and, in extreme cases, this could lead to him becoming aggressive towards others through fear.

Early socialising is important, but do not rush your Miniature Schnauzer into the outside world until he is fully protected by his vaccinations. However, early socialisation is crucial, so invite

Take your Miniature Schnauzer out and about, so that he learns to accept all new situations.

lots of people to your home, so that your puppy becomes confident around a whole range of people before he steps out of his front door.

Once your Mini is vaccinated, you can start to take him for very short walks outdoors. This will allow him to become accustomed to traffic, and to other people and animals.

A good starting point is to take your Mini for short car rides. Always make sure he is secure in the car (either put him in a crate, or fix him to a special safety car harness for dogs), and remember that your dog must never be left in a car, whatever the weather.

Take your Mini for walks along local streets, and to the shops. Only take your dog to a shopping area for the purposes of socialisation. If you plan on shopping for any length of time, leave your Mini at home – tying him to a post while you shop is totally irresponsible.

Usually, while walking with your Miniature Schnauzer puppy, people will be fascinated by the lovely little dog with you, and will

TEACHING TRICKS

Miniature Schnauzers enjoy the stimulation of learning new things. Pirouetting for a treat is easy to teach, and your Mini will soon become an enthusiastic performer!

approach you both. Encourage them to talk to and to pet your dog. However, if children approach, always make sure they do not get overexcited – your pup's experiences with children should always be positive, so that he grows up without fearing them.

You will probably meet other dogs on your walks, and, hopefully, they will play quite happily together. This will help your pup to gain confidence.

PUPPY PARTIES

Many vet surgeries run puppy socialisation parties, where pups can meet other pups. If your Mini grows up with positive experiences of other dogs, he will not fear them. At these 'parties' your pup will learn canine body language, and good doggie manners.

TRAINING CLASSES

Obedience classes are for teaching dogs and owners the correct method of training, and how to get your dog to obey your commands. You will be taught heelwork, Sit, Down, and Stay. Both types of training classes are invaluable, not only for puppies, but for owners as well. It's amazing what tricks and simple

methods are used to encourage puppies to do what you want them to do, instead of what they want to do.

You can usually find a list of these classes advertised in your local pet shop or veterinary surgery.

ADVANCED TRAINING

Ring-training is aimed at people wishing to show their dogs, but it can be useful training for any puppy and his owner.

The purpose of these lessons is to get a puppy used to standing on a table, allowing a person to look at his mouth and feel his body (of particular value when visiting a vet). He will also learn to walk properly on a lead.

Agility is a fun sport for dog and owner alike.

5 *Adult Care*

Very often, you hear the expression that a dog is 'man's best friend'. Unfortunately, we are not always the dog's best friend. Many Miniature Schnauzers are overweight, underexercised or underfed. Some are allowed to stray or are kept in unsuitable conditions. Many people just don't take the trouble and time to find out about owning dogs and keeping them healthy.

DIET

Most adult Miniature Schnauzers will eat anything, but they will be happier and healthier if fed a balanced diet. We all have different ideas about the best diet for our dogs; some people wouldn't dream of feeding a complete dry food, while others wouldn't feed anything else.

You must remember that dogs are like people, and what suits one

Keep to a strict feeding regime so your Miniature Schnauzer does not become overweight.

will not suit another. A good guide to the health of your dog is his general condition – he should have bright eyes, a healthy coat and solid motions.

Some dogs are good converters of food, while others are inefficient and become over-weight. An active dog can eat far more than a lazy one of the same size. It is much easier to put weight on a dog than to take it off, so, if your dog has a tendency to put on weight, feed him less. Miniature Schnauzers are a sturdy, robust dog, but should always have a waistline.

FEEDING SCRAPS

Dogs are, by nature, carnivores (meat eaters), but now they are domesticated and dependent on man, they can thrive on a varied diet.

I can remember my grand-mother feeding scraps to her dog, who seemed to be healthy and who lived to a ripe old age, but nowadays food is prepared differently and mostly processed, so the food values are not the same.

Today, scraps should not be fed, unless added to the main diet as a treat. But be careful that your dog doesn't go on hunger strike when there are no scraps in his dinner!

It is better never to start giving your dog scraps from the table. It leads to bad manners, and constant begging by your dog could be embarrassing if you have guests for dinner. It is best to use treats only for training and as a special, occasional reward.

MEAT

Some breeders feed meat or green tripe (cow's stomach cleaned and chopped). The smell of green tripe is quite strong, but, mixed with a good-quality wholemeal biscuit, adult dogs seem to love it.

You may find you will need to add a little fish oil, and a vitamin and mineral supplement.

CANNED

If you prefer to feed a canned meat rather than fresh, read the label to see if your dog will need extra supplements. To keep your dog in good health, he needs proteins, carbohydrates, fats, minerals, vitamins and trace elements.

COMPLETE

There are plenty of dry complete foods available, but these are only as good as their contents, so buy a reputable brand and read the label to see what ingredients are included. Feed only in accordance with the instructions.

EXERCISE

All dogs should have exercise, even if it's only in your garden, chasing a ball. One thing to remember: don't exercise your dog immediately after feeding; wait at least 30 minutes. In hot weather, exercise your dog in the early morning or late afternoon when it's cooler.

Most dogs should have 30 minutes of free-running exercise every day. Whether this is in your back garden or in a park doesn't really matter, though your dog will enjoy a change of scenery.

One way of spicing up your dog's exercise periods is to teach him to retrieve a ball; or you could hide a couple of biscuits in your garden for him to search out.

If your Mini enjoys swimming, you must be cautious as to where you allow your dog to have a dip. Rivers can be fast-flowing and dangerous, or can contain broken glass or other dangerous debris.

Regular outings, and play sessions in the garden, provide a varied exercise routine.

Never allow your Mini to venture on to the ice, or your dog could break through into the freezing water beneath.

VETERAN CARE

Miniature Schnauzers are generally a healthy breed, living to an average of 14 years. But, as your dog gets older, you will gradually notice certain changes – perhaps he will become a little stiff, or his coat may become thinner. Make sure you do not overexercise him. Your Mini will know how far he wants to walk; when he tires, take him straight home.

If you notice any change in your dog (whether he has bad breath, loses his appetite, drinks more, or becomes stiff etc.), take him to a vet for the necessary treatment.

VETERAN DIET

When your dog becomes a veteran and is less active, his nutritional needs will be different. He won't require such a high level of protein, minerals and calories, but will require a higher content of vitamins and fibre. If you feed your dog once a day, it may be better for his digestion if you now feed two smaller meals a day.

If you are unfortunate enough to have a fussy eater, it can be heartbreaking trying to coax him to eat. Try to be firm, and don't show him that you are anxious, or he will sense this and will dig his heels in even more. Pick up any leftover food and throw it away; start again several hours later, or the next day.

Sometimes, the awareness of another animal ready to eat his food can be a stimulant.

EUTHANASIA

It is a sad fact of life that, sometimes, we have to decide to put our pets to sleep.

If your Mini is suffering, and the vet is not able to relieve the dog's pain, then you must consider your pet's quality of life. The kindest thing you can do is to let your dog be put to sleep to relieve his pain and to allow him to die peacefully and in dignity.

In all instances, talk to your vet who will be able to help you reach a decision which is in your Mini's best interests.

6 *Grooming*

Every owner of a Miniature Schnauzer should have a basic knowledge of grooming. This will enable you to take care of your dog at home or at least to keep him presentable between trips to the beauty parlour. Looking after your Mini should be a pleasant experience for you and your dog.

Miniature Schnauzers require a lot of attention to their grooming and wellbeing. Unlike short-haired breeds, they do not moult, but they have a harsh topcoat with a soft undercoat.

The topcoat should be hand-stripped to remain harsh, which is a must if you intend to show a Miniature Schnauzer. Most pet owners opt to have the coat clipped.

Whether you intend to trim or strip your Mini, or send him to a beauty parlour, regular grooming is essential. You will also need to trim your dog's nails, clean his teeth, and remove hair from his ears.

Whatever method you choose, the Miniature Schnauzer should have the same appearance: long beard, bushy eyebrows, profuse leg hair, and a coat about half an inch long (harsh if stripped, soft if clipped).

Head, ears, cheeks, front (i.e. chest), and belly should be short, blending in the hair where necessary. This is done by using thinning scissors, blending the long hair of the neck, the shorter hair on the throat/cheeks, and the hair on the back legs and bottom.

PUPPY GROOMING

Grooming your dog on a daily basis doesn't have to be a marathon.

To begin with, you will have to convince your puppy that you are not trying to harm him. Each day, pick a time when your puppy is relaxed. Grooming should be a gradual process and eventually

Accustom your puppy to being groomed so that he learns to enjoy the attention.

As the pup becomes more confident, try grooming his whiskers and beard.

your puppy will realise it is not a bad experience.

At first, your pup could be a little nervous and confused, wondering what you are trying to do to him. But with patience and perseverance, you will gain your puppy's confidence.

Stand him on a non-slip mat on a table. Never leave your Mini on the table unattended. He could

jump off the table and seriously hurt himself. Gently comb his beard and leg hair. The breeder may have groomed your puppy; if not, he will object, and will probably try to bite the comb.

If you manage a couple of strokes without your puppy objecting too much, give him lots of praise, and finish the session for that day.

Your puppy must always associate grooming with a pleasant experience, not something to be afraid of.

REMOVING THE PUPPY COAT

If your puppy has a long, fluffy coat, start work on it as soon as possible.

You can use a stripping stone to remove as much of the hair as possible. By taking out the fluffy puppy coat, you will encourage the harsher coat to come through.

You can also try weaving an elastic band in and out of the teeth of your comb. When you then comb the hair on the body, the rubber will grip the hair, and much of the puppy coat can be removed.

ADULT COAT CARE

COMBING

The best type of comb to use is a metal one, with approximately 20 wide teeth and 40 narrow teeth.

If your Mini has any knots, tease them out gently; don't pull on them or you will hurt your dog. Make sure you comb down to the skin, not just the surface of the hair. Pay particular attention to the area underneath the legs, especially the front legs.

If you have a dog, the belly may get stained and sticky when he urinates, so wash this area first. If you comb your Mini every day, you should not have any difficulty dealing with knots.

EYEBROWS

A lot of people find trimming the head a little difficult, but it's quite straightforward. The length of the eyebrows, as long as the shape is correct, can be almost to the end of the nose or short (half-way down the nose). The area between the eyes should be clear of hair.

To shape the eyebrows, stand behind your dog. Holding the head steady with one hand, comb the eyebrows forward. Using a pair of straight scissors, cut from the outer corner of the eye to the middle of the nose.

BEARD

Many people leave far too much hair at the outer corner of the eyes, spoiling the shape of the head. When trimming the cheeks, you should follow the line from the corner of the eye to the corner of the mouth. Then trim the beard accordingly.

Always remember that, when trimmed correctly, your dog's head should have a similar shape to a housebrick.

1. Follow the line from the corner of the eye to the corner of the mouth.

2. With experience, you will learn the correct length of eyebrows and beard.

3. The front legs will need to be tidied.

4. Work on a smooth outline for the undercarriage.

5. Continue working down the hindquarters.

6. The neat and tidy appearance you are aiming for.

EARS

The hair on the ears should be short. With pepper-and-salts, it can either be clipped or stripped. If you opt for clipping the ears on blacks, or black-and-silvers, the hair on the ear will eventually change colour, so always strip this part of the dog.

When stripping the ear hair, always go with the grain of the hair, never against it. The only part of the ear that you can clip is underneath the ear flap.

CLIPPING

If you wish to trim your Mini, you will require a pair of clippers, either electric or hand shears.

The clippers should have two different blades: short for the cheeks, head, ears, underneath the body and rear, and medium for the chest. Use a skip tooth blade, which has two lengths of teeth to allow a longer length on the body.

When you use clippers for the first time, make sure you hold the blade flat to the dog's skin. You could try practising on your own arm (remember to turn the clippers off for this). You will feel the difference when holding the blade flat, as opposed to at an angle.

When clipping, always go with

When clipping, always go with the grain of the coat.

the grain of the coat, not against it, particularly on the body. The only time you should trim against the grain is on the cheeks and throat.

When clipping along the back, you may find it easier to have the dog standing with his head away from you and the rear nearest to you.

To clip the sides, turn the dog so he stands sideways to you, then turn the dog around to do the other side.

I clip my older dogs, and, to preserve any harsh coat they have, I rake all undercoat out before using the clippers. The dog's coat won't be as harsh as it should be, but at least my dogs have retained the banded hair, which gives them the unique individual pepper-and-salt colouring.

Continual clipping of blacks, or black-and-silvers, will fade the colour. Rather, they should be hand-stripped.

STRIPPING/RAKING

Stripping the coat removes the harsh topcoat hair from your dog. Raking removes the undercoat (the fine hair beneath the

A medium stripping knife is used on the topcoat.

topcoat). When the undercoat is removed, the harsh topcoat will appear tighter to the dog's body.

Stripping the coat is something that will have to be done if you intend to show your Mini, as a harsh coat is required in the ring.

There are many stripping knives available from most pet stores. A fine knife is used to remove the undercoat, and a medium knife to shorten and remove the topcoat.

UNDERCOAT
To remove all the undercoat, stand your dog so he is looking away from you, rear end nearest to you. Hold the skin taut a few inches in front of the area you want to strip or rake. This is to ensure that the stripping knife will not accidentally catch any excess skin.

Hold the stripping knife flat against the dog's body, and pull the blade towards you (this is assuming you are right-handed). Take your time and don't be frightened of making a mistake – it will grow again. By raking out the undercoat, you will be encouraging the harsh hair to grow through.

TOPCOAT
To strip the topcoat, you will hold the knife at a different angle, so that you can grab some hair between the knife head and your thumb, and pull it towards you. As with clipping, you should always go with the grain of the hair. To make stripping the sides of the dog easier, lie your Mini on his side – he will be more relaxed this way.

GENERAL CHECKS

TEETH
Once your Mini has cut his second (adult) teeth, begin to brush his teeth every day. (See Chapter Three.)

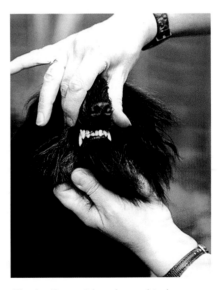

The teeth must be cleaned to keep them free from tartar.

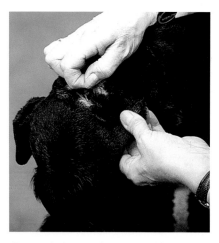

Excess hair must be removed from the ear canal.

EARS

You will need to inspect your Mini's ears, removing hair to help prevent infections.

All dogs should have the excess wax cleaned out. Use a good brand of ear cleaner (your vet will advise) and wipe with cotton wool (cotton). Never probe too deep into the dog's ear. With a puppy, who may not be used to standing on a grooming table, you may find it more convenient to do this while the pup is on your lap.

Use a pair of blunt-ended tweezers. Lift your Mini's ear, and inspect inside. There should be no hair growing from the ear canal. Any visible excess hair should be gently pulled out with the tweezers.

To prevent the area becoming sore, take a small amount at a time – just a few hairs – then massage the ear and let your Mini rest. Give a treat as a reward for being good.

FEET

Next, inspect your Mini's feet. Toenails must be trimmed and filed, and the hair in between the pads should be trimmed. A puppy's toenails seem to grow at a very fast rate, so inspect these every week and trim off the tips.

Be careful not to cut off too

Take care to trim just the tips of the nails.

Regular grooming sessions will keep your Miniature Schnauzer in tip-top condition.

much, as you may cut the quick and cause bleeding. Plus, your Miniature Schnauzer will be in great pain, and may learn to hate having his feet touched.

If the hair is allowed to grow between the pads, then mud etc. could stick to the hair and cause your Mini problems when he walks.

You might find it more convenient to check your Mini puppy's feet when he is on your lap, but an adult dog can have his feet checked while he is on a grooming table.

7 Showing Your Miniature Schnauzer

The first organisation founded to authorise canine activities and to maintain records of shows was the Kennel Club, founded in 1873 in London. The American Kennel Club, founded in 1884, followed examples already in practice by the Kennel Club in England.

Nowadays, dogs are categorised in different Groups. These may vary slightly from one country to another. In England, the Kennel Club has placed the Miniature Schnauzer in the Utility Group, while, in America, it is placed in the Terrier Group.

THE BREED STANDARD

A Breed Standard is the written description of the features for pure-bred dogs, written by the kennel clubs/breed clubs in their respective countries. The Standard represents a balanced and typical Miniature Schnauzer. Judges use this as a model against which to compare class entrants at a show – the dog closest to the Standard wins.

You may find reading the Breed Standard useful when selecting a puppy, or if you think you might like to start showing. Contact your national kennel club for a copy of the Standard.

The following explains the key points of the ideal Miniature Schnauzer.

TEMPERAMENT

This is what makes the Miniature Schnauzer such a delight. He is alert, reliable and intelligent – the ideal companion dog.

GENERAL APPEARANCE

The Miniature Schnauzer should be a sturdily-built, robust little dog, yet sinewy and nearly square (the length of the body being equal to the height at the shoulders).

The Miniature Schnauzer is a robust little dog with a keen, alert expression.

His expression should be keen, intelligent, and he should have an alert attitude.

The Miniature Schnauzer should never be toyish or fine-boned, neither should he be described as racy or coarse (i.e. lacking refinement). Rather, he should be smart and stylish, adaptable, and well balanced.

The Miniature Schnauzer should never appear terrier-ish or 'cloddy'. He should not be low, thick-set, or comparatively heavy.

HEAD
The shape of the Miniature Schnauzer's head should resemble a housebrick, or rectangle, slightly narrowing from the ears to the eyes, and again from the eyes to the tip of the nose.

The forehead should be wrinkle-free, and the top part of the head moderately broad between the ears.

He should have a medium stop – i.e. a slight step from the skull down the bridge of the nose. This

The Mini's head should resemble a housebrick in shape.

indentation between the eyes helps to accentuate the breed's characteristic eyebrows.

EARS

The ears should be a neat V-shape, set quite high on the head and falling forward towards the temple.

EYES

The eyes must be dark and oval. Round, light eyes detract from the quizzical expression that Minis have.

MOUTH

The mouth should end in a blunt line – it should not be pointed or 'snipey'. The teeth should be a perfect scissor-bite, meaning the top teeth closely overlap the bottom teeth.

NECK

The Miniature Schnauzer's neck should be moderately long, strong and slightly arched. The skin should be close to the throat, and the neck should be set cleanly on his shoulders.

FOREQUARTERS

The neck is of moderate length and slightly arched. It flows into the back, giving the Mini an elegant and proud look.

BODY

Everything about the Miniature Schnauzer is moderate, nothing is exaggerated. The body should be short and compact, square, and well balanced.

The chest should be moderately broad and deep, reaching at least to the elbow, and the ribs should form a gentle curve; they should be neither flat nor round.

We are looking for a firm, well-developed body that isn't too thin (no protruding ribs) and does not carry too much fat. Minis should possess a waistline. When viewed in profile, you should be able to just see the breastbone protruding a little in front of the dog's legs.

The topline of the back is strong and straight, slightly higher at the shoulder, sloping gently to the tail. A dog whose back curves like a Whippet, or a dog whose topline dips in the middle, is not acceptable and should be avoided.

TAIL

The tail, which is customarily docked to three joints, should not be low down, but set high, perpendicular to the back. This gives a straight and proud appearance.

LEGS

The Mini's length of foreleg from the elbow to the ground should be equal to the depth of the chest, and this will contribute to the square appearance required.

Observed from all angles, the bone should be strong, the legs straight. The elbows should point directly backwards and be close to the body.

The hindlegs should be nicely angled, bending at the stifle (knee joint). The hocks (the rear ankles) should be straight and vertical to the ground. Correct angulation and muscle tone will ensure sound movement.

The body is compact and balanced.

FEET

Short, round and cat-like, the feet should be compact with closely arched toes, dark nails, and firm black pads. All feet should point forward.

GAIT/MOVEMENT

The Miniature Schnauzer's movement should be free-flowing, the front legs reaching forward in a straight line, with the hindlegs driving the dog forward.

The back foot should move into the spot which the front foot has left. The topline should remain level while the dog moves.

Hackney action (where the front legs high-step like a horse), or rolling, short, stilted stepping, are both unacceptable.

COAT

The coat should be harsh, wiry and short enough for smartness. The undercoat should be dense.

The coat should be close and short on the neck and shoulders, the ears, and the skull. The hair on the legs is harsh. The furnishings (the leg hair, beard and skirt) should be fairly thick but not silky.

COLOUR

Pure black, black-and-silver, or pepper-and-salt (in even

The free-flowing gait which is typical of the Miniature Schnauzer.

proportions). All pepper-and-salt colours should be in even proportions.

Black-and-silver markings should be as follows: solid black with silver markings on eyebrow, muzzle, chest and brisket and on the forelegs below the point of elbow, on the inside of the hindlegs below the stifle joint, on the vent, and under the tail.

SIZE

The ideal height for dogs should be 35.6 cms (14 inches) and for bitches 33 cms (13 inches) at the withers.

Minis that are too small or that have a 'toyish' appearance are not typical, and are undesirable.

AMERICAN DIFFERENCES

The American Kennel Club Breed Standard for Miniature Schnauzers is slightly different to the British one.

In America, the ears can be cropped, so the ear stands erect. If cropped, they should be identical in shape and length, with pointed tips.

The ears should not be exaggerated in length, and should be in balance with the head, set high on the skull.

When uncropped, the ears should be small and V-shaped, folding close to the skull.

GETTING STARTED

Selecting a puppy to show is extremely difficult; no-one can guarantee what an eight-week-old pup will look like as an adult.

Experienced, reputable breeders should be able to advise you on which puppy should not be shown, but at eight weeks so

many things can go wrong as the puppy grows.

If you are lucky enough to have picked a Mini that is worthy of being shown, you have to consider the hard work involved preparing a Miniature Schnauzer for the show ring.

Competing against professionals or the more experienced owners can be a little daunting, but with dedication and perseverance a newcomer can do very well. Remember, everyone has to start somewhere.

BEST PRESENTATION

A Miniature Schnauzer needs trimming and stripping to obtain the correct Schnauzer appearance and harsh coat.

In the UK, most owners trim and handle their own dogs at shows, so consider the hard work, patience and knowledge of show regulations that is needed.

In America, the services of professional handlers are sometimes used. These handlers are experts, and know all the tricks for getting the best out of a dog. But the services of professionals are not essential, and amateurs are capable of exhibiting their dogs.

What is important to remember, whether you are competing at a small show or an important Championship show, is that your dog should always look his best. Show dogs should be kept in top condition. In addition, good nature is all-important – a dog's temperament and showmanship can make or break a show career.

NATURAL SHOW DOG

Miniature Schnauzers are no different to any other breed. Some will take to showing and will walk around the ring, almost saying to the judges "Hey, look at me! I'm the greatest."; others have little ring presence and hate being shown.

With correct socialisation, excellent grooming, and clever, confident handling, however, even a mediocre dog can do reasonably well in the show ring.

LEARNING GAIT

The gait is the pattern of footsteps and pace at which you move your dog around the ring.

The Miniature Schnauzer's movement should be free-flowing, and so he should not be shown on a short lead. If the lead is too tight and you pull the dog up off his front feet, it will shorten his step and ruin his gait.

Your local ring-training class will help you to practise perfecting your dog's gait.

HANDLING

If you are handling your dog yourself, then you may find it useful to go along to your local ring-training class, as good dogs can be ruined by bad handling. A class will help to boost your confidence, and to improve your handling skills.

Handling is an art in itself. You need to have confidence and an understanding of what is required from the handler. Make it fun; don't let your dog get bored.

Visit some shows, and watch the handlers. You will notice different styles of handling – some are natural, while some prefer their dogs to be like little robots, standing stock still. Decide what is best for your dog, and try to nurture a style suitable to you both.

THE SHOW STANCE

You will need to accomplish the art of stacking your Mini in the correct stance. Visit a couple of shows and watch how the exhibitors stack or stand their Minis.

When you practise, stand in front of a mirror, so that you have the same view as a judge. The head should arch and flow into the shoulders.

Look at the difference to the dog's overall appearance when you stand your dog with his head looking up, or when his head looks downwards.

Practise a little each day, encouraging your dog to stand still for a few seconds. Bestow lots of praise when your dog doesn't move, and your Mini will soon learn what is expected of him.

The dog is placed in the correct position to show himself off to maximum advantage.

PUPPY CLASS

Dogs can be shown in puppy classes at the age of six months, so you should have started the training and socialisation well in advance.

Your Mini should be accustomed to being handled and having his teeth examined. Some judges will require you to open the dog's mouth, so make sure you are adept at doing this.

By six months of age, your Mini should be travelling in the car, and meeting other people and dogs with confidence.

RULES

Whatever country you live in, it is advisable to contact your own

With practice, you and your dog will become polished performers in the show ring.

Kennel Club to find out what rules and regulations should be adhered to.

Join a breed club and attend a couple of shows. Breed shows are where you will meet dedicated enthusiasts of the Miniature Schnauzer, and you should be able to glean enough information on trimming, stripping and handling Minis.

Of course, you will also make lots of new friends, who all share your love of the breed.

8 *Health Care*

The Miniature Schnauzer is generally a healthy breed, and, apart from his annual check-up and booster vaccinations, your dog should lead a fairly trouble-free life.

Always be aware of any changes in your dog's eating and drinking habits, and in his behaviour. Also keep a close eye on his bowel movements as these can sometimes indicate when something is wrong.

Never allow symptoms to continue unchecked for any length of time – the moment you notice anything different about your Miniature Schnauzer, you should consult a vet.

ADMINISTERING MEDICINE

At some point during your dog's life, you will have to give your dog medicine. It can be daunting at first, but you will become more confident with experience.

Liquid is relatively easy to administer. Ask your vet for a syringe, which will be marked with the dosage. Arrange for a friend to hold the dog still. Insert a finger into the side of the dog's lips, and pull slightly apart and outwards to form a little pocket. Tilt the head slightly backwards and slowly syringe the liquid into the corner of the mouth. Keep the dog's mouth shut, and gently rub the throat to make sure he has swallowed.

Tablets are a little more difficult. Some owners crush the tablet and put it in food, or wrap the tablet in meat. Ask your vet's advice beforehand, as some medicines must not be given with food.

Open the dog's mouth, tilt the head slightly backwards and drop the tablet or capsule right to the back of the dog's throat. Close the mouth and massage the throat to encourage him to swallow.

Initially, the puppy receives immunity from his dam. This is replaced with vaccination.

PREVENTATIVE CARE

VACCINATIONS
There are various vaccinations which your puppy will need, and which your adult dog will need to be regularly boosted with.

CANINE DISTEMPER
A highly, infectious viral disease which is still a prime cause of death in non-vaccinated puppies. The disease is transmitted through moisture droplets, and dogs usually pick it up while sniffing where infected dogs have been.

Symptoms include: a wet cough, diarrhoea, high temperature, loss of appetite, sore eyes, and a runny nose.

In some variants, the nose and foot pads become hard and cracked. Severe cases can lead to pneumonia, fits, muscle spasms and paralysis.

CANINE HEPATITIS
A virus which can attack the liver, kidneys, eyes and lungs of infected dogs. It is spread by direct contact with infected urine, saliva or faeces. Symptoms include: fever, abdominal pain, diarrhoea and vomiting.

LEPTOSPIROSIS
A bacterial disease picked up from the infected urine of rats, causing kidney and liver failure. Symptoms include: high temperature, depression, severe thirst, lethargy, vomiting and jaundice.

CANINE PARVOVIRUS
A virus transmitted by contact with infected faeces, it can also be carried on the dog's hair, feet, and feeding utensils. The virus is difficult to eliminate, and can persist in the environment for many months.

Dogs of all ages can become infected, but puppies are particularly susceptible to the disease.

Symptoms include: sudden onset of vomiting, high temperature, and foul-smelling, bloody diarrhoea. Prompt attention is needed as dogs rapidly dehydrate, may collapse, and can

die within 24 hours of the symptoms appearing.

KENNEL COUGH
A highly contagious disease caused by a variety of infectious agents, including canine parainfluenza virus and the Bordetella bacterium. It is passed on by breathing in contaminated airborne droplets or through direct contact with infected dogs.

Symptoms include: a harsh, dry cough without mucus or phlegm, and gagging or retching. The severity differs and may last a few days or weeks.

If you think your dog may be infected with kennel cough, do not take him into the vet's surgery; instead, make arrangements for your vet to treat your dog in isolation.

WORMING YOUR MINI
Hopefully, the breeder will have started your puppy's worming programme, and it is important to continue with the procedure and ensure your Mini receives all the worming doses during puppyhood and then regularly throughout his life (ask your vet for details).

ROUNDWORM
Roundworms are found in the intestines of dogs, and are a major hygienic concern because they can be transmitted to humans. They look like pieces of string or noodles. Puppies which are heavily infested with roundworms develop pot bellies and possibly sickness or diarrhoea. Adults rarely show symptoms, but can still be affected.

TAPEWORM
The main tapeworm affecting dogs is called *Dipylidium caninum* and is carried by the flea. Tapeworm segments look like flat grains of rice. They are sometimes noticed around the anus and in the motions of infected dogs. These segments contain eggs.

Tapeworm passes from dog to dog via the flea (and the dog then accidentally eats the flea while grooming). So, keeping your dogs free of fleas is an excellent way of protecting against tapeworm.

ACCIDENTS

BEE STINGS
Miniature Schnauzers love to chase bees and wasps, but a single sting will produce intense local pain with some swelling. Stings are usually in or around the mouth, resulting in increased

salivation, and the dog pawing at his mouth.

Stings on the skin will cause the dog to lick the site. If the tongue is stung, it can swell to the extent that it blocks the passage of air through the back of the throat.

The site of the sting should be examined, and, if the sting is still present, it should be carefully removed with a pair of tweezers. A sting will only be present if it was a bee sting. Application of

antihistamine is valuable. If the sting is in the mouth, wash out with sodium bicarbonate solution.

Some dogs are allergic to the sting and go into a state of severe shock and collapse, requiring immediate veterinary treatment.

If there is a lot of swelling in the mouth and/or difficulty in breathing or if the dog seems in shock and collapsed, a veterinary surgeon should be contacted immediately. A dog that appears to be choking should be laid on its side, with the tongue pulled well forward out of the mouth.

Any dog in shock should be maintained in a horizontal position and kept warm. If the dog shows signs of wanting to drink, let him.

HEATSTROKE

Dogs left in cars can suffer heatstroke and die. Never leave your dog unattended in a car – whatever the weather. Parking in the shade offers no protection.

A dog with heatstroke will be weak, panting, and near collapse. He may vomit and his temperature will be very high. This is an acute emergency and the dog's temperature must be lowered as soon as possible.

Use cold, wet towels or immerse the dog in cold water. Once the dog shows signs of recovery, keep him cool and encourage him to drink.

CUTS

Minor cuts should be cleansed, and a mild antiseptic should be applied. Cover with a bandage, but make sure it is not too tight, or it may stop the circulation. Any deep cuts, or any profuse bleeding, should receive veterinary attention at once.

BURNS

Treat with cold, wet compresses until you can get your dog to a veterinary surgeon.

BREED-PRONE CONDITIONS

EYE CONDITIONS

Unfortunately, hereditary problems occur in many breeds and Miniature Schnauzers are not without theirs. Miniature Schnauzers are affected by cataracts and progressive retinal atrophy (PRA).

Many owners and breeders are wary of the mention of hereditary problems, but responsible custodians of our lovely breed will always do their very best to help eradicate any inherited problems.

To help overcome these horrible inherited eye problems, it is imperative that all Miniature Schnauzers are eye-tested annually and that breeding stock is eye-tested before mating.

If you are unfortunate enough to own a Miniature Schnauzer diagnosed with an eye problem, you should inform the breeder and the clubs. It is not a crime, and any information received will help in eradicating these eye problems.

Because cataracts and generalised progressive retinal

atrophy (GPRA), are inherited by a recessive gene, it is not possible to identify the carriers of the gene, unless a time-consuming and sometimes heartbreaking test-mating programme is pursued.

CATARACTS

Both hereditary and congenital hereditary cataracts are found in Miniature Schnauzers.

Hereditary cataracts may be detected from six months of age upwards, some even later than three years. Congenital hereditary cataract can be detected at six to eight weeks of age.

Apart from the undesirable perpetuation of abnormalities within breeding lines, inherited cataracts progress to produce visual impairment and blindness.

Both types are reported to be bilateral (affects both eyes) and caused by an autosomal recessive gene (a genetic disorder that appears only in offspring that have received two copies of the mutant gene, one from each parent).

GPRA

Generalised progressive retinal atrophy is not detectable in Miniature Schnauzers until three years of age. Most owners will notice a loss of night vision,

With good care, your Miniature Schnauzer will live a long and healthy life.

especially when the dog is in unfamiliar surroundings. The condition will progress to total blindness. An autosomal recessive gene causes this condition.

HAEMORRHAGIC GASTROENTERITIS

This virus can strike at any time, and very quickly. Nobody seems to know where a dog contracts the disease, but prompt action must be taken.

The symptoms are very similar to parvovirus: vomiting, bloody diarrhoea, weight loss and profound dehydration.

Lots of water with a little glucose should be given to combat the fluid loss, but I cannot emphasise enough the importance of seeking immediate veterinary help.

KIDNEY FAILURE

Most dogs with renal failure drink more and urinate more. They may become anorexic and lethargic, and may lose weight. Vomiting, diarrhoea and depression may also be experienced. Your vet will be able to advise you on a suitable way of managing the problem.

DIABETES

The symptoms of diabetes are very similar to those for kidney failure. Examination by your dog's vet will determine whether your dog is diabetic.

ADDISON'S DISEASE

This is also known as hypoadrenocorticism, where a dog produces too much adrenal hormone.

Dogs suffering from Addison's can be misdiagnosed as having kidney disease or digestive disorders. It usually causes depression, a diminished appetite, vomiting, and loose stools.

CUSHING'S DISEASE

This is known as hyperadrenocorticism, where the dog produces too much cortisol. It affects different dogs in different ways.

Symptoms include increased thirst, thinning hair/hair loss, exercise intolerance, and muscle weakness.

SCHNAUZER BUMPS

These are hard, scabby lesions (comodomes) which occur along the top of the back. A dog that has greasy, dry or smelly skin can be described as seborrhoeic (a term used for a rash, eczema etc.). There are dozens of skin diseases that can result in seborrhoea, or, to give it the correct name, keratinization.

The shedding of dead skin speeds up in a dog with keratinization and causes the skin to become greasy, smelly and scaling.

This process can be caused by many problems, including allergies, hormonal or nutritional imbalances, immune problems, or hereditary defects such as thyroid conditions.

There is no specific treatment for seborrhoea, but, if diagnosed correctly, then medicated shampoos are likely to be necessary.